Tropical Living

The Deutsche Nationalbibliothek lists this publication in the Deutsche Nationalbibliografie; detailed bibliographic data are available on the Internet at http://dnb.dnb.de

ISBN 978-3-03768-179-4
© 2015 by Braun Publishing AG
www.braun-publishing.ch

1st edition 2015

Selection of projects and layout: Manuela Roth
Text editing and translation: Judith Vonberg
Editorial staff: Benjamin Langer
Art direction: Michaela Prinz, Berlin

Manuela Roth

Tropical Living

Dream Houses at Exotic Places

BRAUN

Contents

Preface

It's not only when daily life snaps at our heels and we find ourselves scampering from one appointment to the next that we dream of a more relaxed life somewhere in the South Seas. Somewhere far away from our everyday responsibilities and the traffic and the noise of the city. We dream of a simple life lived among palm trees, in harmony with nature. We dream of the tropics – paradise on earth. Wishing ourselves there, we dream of palms, crystal clear waters, unending beaches, sunshine. Of tropical rainforests, lush vegetation and unusual animals – breathtaking natural beauty.

The regions around the equator experience extreme weather conditions. Although the temperatures are constant throughout the year, there are long rainy seasons. The highest rainfall worldwide occurs in the tropics. The architecture, especially residential architecture, is responsive to these specialized climatic conditions. Carefully selected for this volume, the featured houses pay tribute to the natural world in unique ways, but without compromising on design and luxury. Their architects blur the boundaries between interior and exterior, open the living areas to the outside world and offer an invitation to become a part of nature. Using natural materials such as wood and stone they create comfortable spaces in which residents can shelter from sun and rain while observing and enjoying breathtaking views of tropical flora and fauna.

From the Caribbean to Brazil, from the Seychelles to Vietnam: every country and region is unique. Yet they share the same need for respectful treatment of nature and an awareness of humanity's responsibility for the earth. The houses presented in this book showcase the breadth of creativity in tropical architecture, whether an urban or jungle weekend retreat, a functional family home, a tree house in harmony with nature or a grand, luxurious villa. They all embrace the natural world through their architecture. Ponds and pools offer a welcome chance to cool off, while inner courtyards afford the intimacy that enables the surrounding rooms to be opened to the world.

Contemporary architecture attempts to leave the smallest possible footprint on the earth. An outstanding example is *K House* in Costa Rica: embedded in tropical forest, the house undoubtedly exhibits a sensitive approach to the site. Sustainable adaptability is the watchword – and with its simple, local construction methods and the ingenious utilization of the natural surroundings, this is the perfect realization of the concept. The horizontal structure floats above the floor and rises into the treetops, while a vertical tower offers spectacular views of the surrounding vegetation and sea. Minimalistic but designed with great respect for and attention to the lush vegetation of the garden, the *Cube House* in São Paulo is an impressive urban house. The cube is perforated at strategic places to generate elongated spaces and openings. The generous living area can be completely opened to extend into the garden towards the pool or closed to offer privacy and shade. Breathtaking views over São Paulo can be enjoyed from the large roof terrace. Comprising rough concrete and metallic panels, the façade's colors perfectly echo the adjacent concrete. *The Library House* in India unifies old and new, Indian tradition and globalized modernity. With ample space to breathe, a verandah to watch the falling rain and an interior garden with a pool, this ecologically sensitive house perfectly combines functionality and beauty. From the road you see a striking tiled walkway flanked with wooden columns that traverses a courtyard boasting a tropical fishpond, yellow ochre walls and an ancient swing. Sliding doors and open-plan layouts in the interior create a magnificent and seamless living space. Old and new are also united in *Re-wrapped House* in Singapore. This modernization of a 1970s house is truly unique. The architects from A D Lab studied the structure as a living organism, creating a new living space in harmony with its built and tropical surroundings. The roof was interpreted afresh as the fifth façade, embracing the house and lending it a distinctive character.

Whether beach, tropical forest or urban space, *Tropical Living – Dream Houses at Exotic Places* presents houses that represent a relaxed lifestyle in harmony with nature. Old and new, tradition and modernity, comfort and simplicity, sustainability and contemporary design find unity in unique architectural projects. Browse through this richly illustrated volume and allow yourself to absorb the serenity and beauty of the houses and their precious natural worlds, find your personal paradise and relax your body and soul.

from above to below, from left to right: terrace offers outdoor
living area, sunlit deck, detail stone base

outdoor dining area

Rock House

Miami, Florida, USA

Architect: Max Strang
Architecture
Year of completion: 2004
Gross floor area: 511 m²
Materials used: oolitic lime-
stone, steel, ipe wood, Florida
keystone

Located in Miami's tropical enclave of Coconut Grove, the Rock House has become one of Miami's iconic residences and manifests a seamless merging of architecture and landscape. The entire upper floor is inspired by the tropical designs of the late Sri Lankan architect Geoffrey Bawa. An exposed rusted steel roof provides a modernist edge to the overall esthetic, while local oolitic limestone encloses the lower floor. The pool was excavated amidst the ruins of a small cottage that was formerly on the property. Orchids grow from the low stone foundation walls and occasionally drop flowers into the black bottomed pool. Although technically located in a subtropical climate, Rock House proves that the 'tropics' are alive and well in Miami.

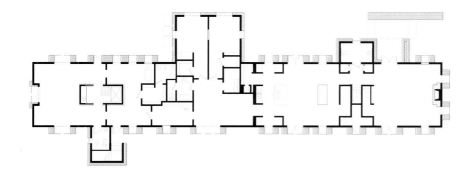

from above to below, from left to right: floor plan, dining area, kitchen, living room

from left to right, from above to below: exterior rear view,
sunlit terrace, cooling pool

from above to below: view from deck to backyard and bay, view from Biscayne Bay

rear view with backyard and pool

Coral Gables Residence

Coral Gables, Florida, USA

Architect: Touzet Studio
Year of completion: 2012
Gross floor area: 566 m²
Materials used: coral rock, simena limestone, American walnut

The apparent conflict between the client's fantasy of a modern home and the city's classically-oriented design code spawned a residence that juxtaposes the traditional and the contemporary in true style. Two modest stone-clad volumes face the city harmonizing perfectly with neighboring architecture. On the opposite side, the true nature of the house and the client's desire for spectacular soaring roofs, glass walls and modern building materials are openly and joyously expressed. The city's requirement of sloping tiled roofs was re-interpreted in a series of sloping planes, their upper surfaces clad in photovoltaic cells, floating above glass walls. Stylish and elegant, this residence is a unique and refreshing example of tropical design.

from above to below, from left to right: ground floor plan, main entrance with steps and façade from limestone, terrace on second floor with view over the bay, front view at night

from above to below: rear view at night, great living room

from above to below, from left to right: view from deck to dining room, master bathroom, terrace on second floor

from above to below: pool deck, second floor plan

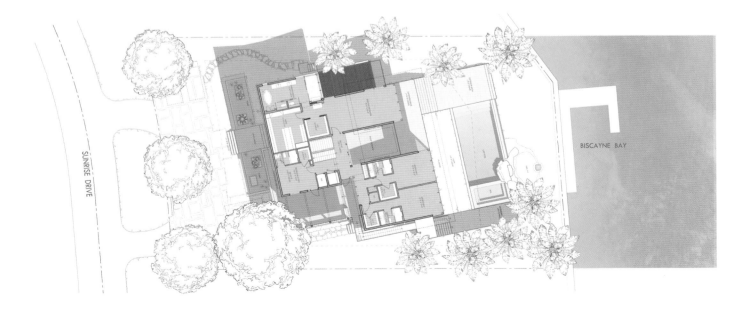

SUNRISE DRIVE

BISCAYNE BAY

exterior with surroundings

exterior view looking north towards the sea

Lavaflow 5

Big Island, Hawaii, USA

Architect: Craig Steely
Architecture
Year of completion: 2012
Gross floor area: 260 m²
Materials used: steel

Simple lines, clean angles and unpretentious design define Lavaflow 5. Walls of varying opacity envelop this elegant home overlooking the stunning Hamakua coastline. Sea and sky are center-stage, the structure a modest but stylish addition to the landscape. Pre-fabricated in San Francisco, the frame was delivered to the site along with an off-the-shelf, self-supporting roof system. It took just five days to erect the frame and roof – an impressive achievement! Protected from strong winds and facing towards the ocean, the interior receives filtered sunlight throughout the day and is passively cooled by cross ventilation. This decidedly simple yet perfectly ingenious structure of steel, concrete and glass is surely the perfect Hawaiian home.

19

from above to below: south façade from inside, sun louvers on
south façade

from left to right, from above to below: master bedroom, entry leads over koi pond, detail entrance with breathtaking view, floor plan

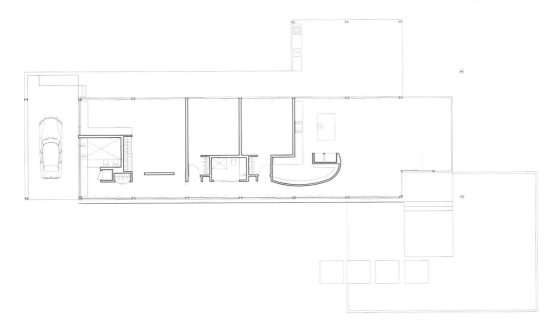

from above to below: villas nestled in green surrounding, view from below towards sun deck

breathtaking view from pool deck

Le Sereno Villas

St. Barthélemy, French West Indies

Architect: Luis Pons Design Lab
Year of completion: 2008
Gross floor area: 604 m²
Materials used: concrete, concrete blocks, stucco, wood, glass

Spacious, simple, airy, and surrounded by stunning ocean views, three contiguous villas at Le Sereno were conceptualized as a series of roofs protecting a generous sundeck. Making use of the various lot levels and incorporating angles into the architecture, each villa offers impressive exterior expanses for sunbathing and entertaining that remain out of sight of neighbors. Ipe wood siding, decks, banisters and trellises wrap the villa with clean horizontal lines, creating a traditional but streamlined contemporary esthetic. Movable slatted screens add a compelling modernist twist to the traditional plantation shutter. These striking dwellings stand as a testament to the power of architectural innovation.

interior view living and dining area

from above to below: interior looking out towards deck and sea,
first floor plan

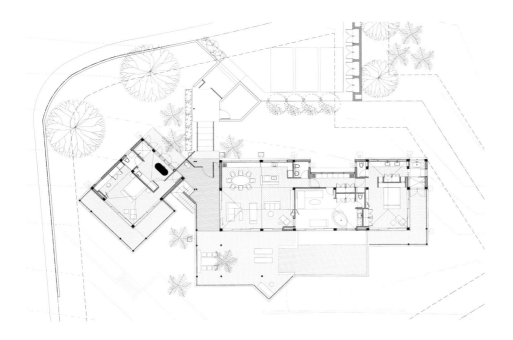

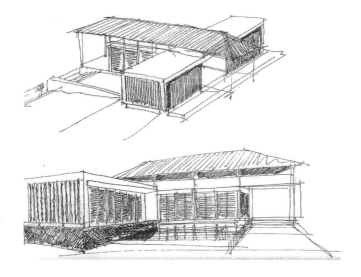

from above to below, from left to right: design sketch exterior, detail garden, outdoor dining area, covered terrace

from left to right, from above to below: pool deck, detail terrace, terrace overlooking the ocean

from above to below: south façade, view from the pool towards
the south façade

open-space living room

Casa Sisal

Acanceh, Yucatán, Mexico

Architect: reyes ríos + larraín arquitectos
Year of completion: 2010
Gross floor area: 200 m²
Materials used: cement blocks, concrete, chukum finish

The name of this spectacular residence evokes the agave plants that were cultivated on the site enclosed by old masonry walls dating back to the late 1800s. Covering an impressive 200 square meters, the two-bedroom, two-bathroom home is used as a rather luxurious guesthouse for the hacienda San Antonio Sacchich. Two large glass walls enclose the central living/kitchen area, sliding back ingeniously to allow the space to become a fabulous extension to the exterior patio and swimming pool. Stunning white stucco envelops the structure, a mixture of white cement and resins from local chukum trees. Originally mastered by the Mayas, this ancient technique yokes the modern design with a proud and ancient architectural heritage.

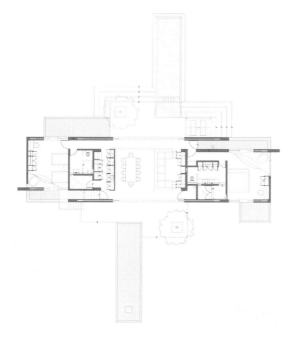

from above to below, from left to right: floor plan, stairs leading to the rooftop terrace, bathroom

from above to below: view from north at dusk,
master bedroom

from above to below, from left to right: pool deck with greened
wall, living area, detail façade

living area opens towards pool deck

Casa Palma Chit

Fraccionamiento Palmaris, Cancún, Mexico

Architect: JC Arquitectura –
Juan Carral
Year of completion: 2011
Gross floor area: 160 m²
Materials used: precast con-
crete, concrete slabs, polished
cement floors

A house for a young family on a small plot? JC Arquitectura met the challenge with relish and the result is
undeniably outstanding! Ingenious planning means that
the living and dining areas, covered terrace and master
bedroom are all north facing and enjoy the tropical Mexican sunlight. The open-plan living area, free of distracting
columns and beams, merges with the garden and small

pool outside, blurring the boundaries of internal and external space. Constructed in just three months from local
precast concrete blocks and slabs, Casa Palma Chit is a
triumph of economy, functionality and sophistication. This
is a residence that exemplifies perfection and simplicity in
tropical design.

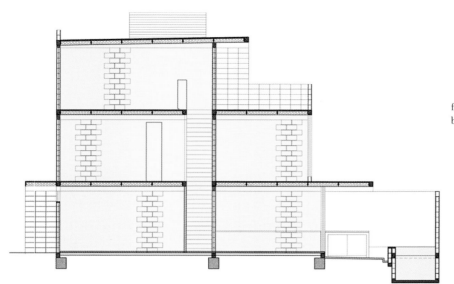

from above to below, from left to right: section, staircase, master bedroom, pool deck

from above to below: dining area, dining area opens towards
kitchen

from above to below, from left to right: living room with colorful
decoration, house from below, terrace with dining area

from above to below, from left to right: house nestled in surroundings, cantilevering volume, staircase to garden

Casa Narigua

El Jonuco, Nuevo León, Mexico

Architect: P+o Architecture (David Pedroza Castañeda)
Year of completion: 2013
Gross floor area: 750 m²
Materials used: colored and gray concrete, glass, wood in structure and flooring, natural stone

Nestled among vegetation on the side of a mountain, Casa Narigua is a spectacular sight. Existing in total harmony with the surrounding ecosystems, the structure is lifted above the tree-tops and divided into zones around groups of old cedar trees. The lucky inhabitants can enjoy magnificent 360-degree views of the mountains and their diverse flora and fauna. Thick walls, flat roofs and timber beams pay tribute to traditional Mexican architecture, their palette humbly complementing the surrounding dramatic landscape. Antique and contemporary furniture, paintings, masks and sculptures are scattered through the interior, generating a sense of timelessness enhanced by the age-old landscape.

from above to below, from left to right: living room with view towards dining area, kitchen with exit to terrace, interior dining area

from left to right, from above to below: staircase, interior view
foyer, sun deck with pool, ground floor plan

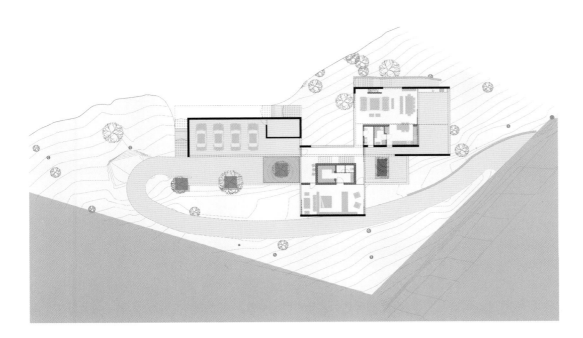

from above to below, from left to right: view of garden with
private beach, roofed terrace, private beach

exterior view from garden

Casa La Punta

Punta Mita, Nayarit, Mexico

Architect: Elías Rizo
Arquitectos
Year of completion: 2012
Gross floor area: 795 m²
Materials used: polished
concrete, Parota wood, natural
stone, stainless steel

Casa La Punta is the home of an unusual client with a keen eye for design. Built in Punta Mita just a few paces from the sea, the house boldly breaks away from traditional local design. Composed of simple, unassuming volumes in constant open dialogue with their context, Casa La Punta may set a new architectural trend in the region! Tropical wooden planks connect the house with the rolling ocean waves, inviting you to cool your feet in the salty spray. A palette of polished concrete, solid Parota wood, natural stone and stainless steel combines the man-made and the natural in perfect visual harmony. Carefully crafted interiors are modestly finished with a meticulous selection of simple wooden furniture.

from above to below, from left to right: living area with open-
air bathtub, open living area, dining area

from above to below: path through garden, private beach with bathtub, design sketch façade

from above to below: terrace with pool, building nestled in the rainforest

swimming pool with stunning view

Casa Torcida

Osa Peninsula, Costa Rica

Architect: SPG Architects
Year of completion: 2008
Gross floor area: 1,672 m²
Materials used: glass, stone, steel, concrete

This spectacular transformation of an abandoned steel and concrete structure is courtesy of SPG Architects. Environmentally sensitive, technologically advanced, and modernist by design, the striking five-level residence is situated on a lush forested mountainside overlooking the Golfo Dulce – a fabulous location. Taking inspiration from the Osa's natural world, SPG juxtaposed bright, tropical colors with the beautifully neutral palette of the building materials to create a harmonious esthetic unity. The colors reflect the abundant flora and fauna that surround the house. Practical yet stylish, indigenous yet modern, this dwelling is an awesome testament to the possibilities inspired by tropical living.

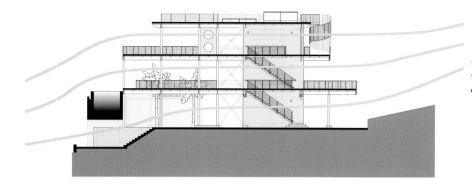

from above to below, from left to right: section with ventilation diagram, terrace with view towards bedrooms, night view, entrance area

from left to right, from above to below: interior view library,
bedroom, kitchen

from above to below: boundaries between inside and outside blur,
horizontally stretched building part

from above to below, from left to right: view from kitchen to
outside dining area, rear façade, living in the treetops

K House

Playa Guiones, Guanacaste, Costa Rica

Architect: Datumzero
Design Office
Year of completion: 2012
Gross floor area: 329 m²
Materials used: concrete,
wood, steel

Located on a demanding site in Costa Rica, K House is the magnificent result of a long and complex design and construction process. Embedded in the thick of the tropics, the residence is an honest and undoubtedly sensitive response to the site. Sustainable adaptability was the key concept – and with its local simple construction methods and ingenious use of the natural context, this dwelling is the perfect manifestation of that idea. The horizontal floating house invades the canopy tree spaces in harmony with local wildlife, while a vertical structure rises spectacularly to provide glorious views of the surroundings. A whimsical external staircase leads to a roof terrace, returning us to the impressive sights and sounds of the dazzling sea.

49

from above to below, from left to right: tower with a view,
house nestled in the wood, strong connection to nature

from left to right, from above to below: outdoor swimming pool, living room with view towards kitchen, living area, floor plan upper level

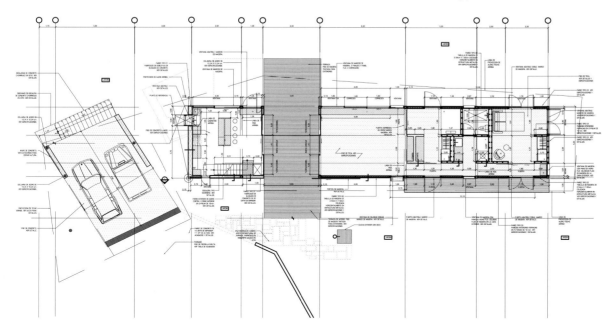

library pavilion

walkway to library pavilion

Casa Kiké

Cahuita, Costa Rica

Architect: Gianni Botsford Architects
Year of completion: 2007
Gross floor area: 180 m²
Materials used: timber (Cachà, laurel), corrugated iron, glass louvres

Ingenious yet modest, traditional yet contemporary, Casa Kiké stands at the forefront of architectural enterprise. Exploiting the untapped potential of the parallelogram, the dwelling comprises two such forms, their glazed ends cleverly twisted away from the meridian so as to catch the welcome northerly sea breezes and provide shade from the tropical sun. Built on 1.2-meter piles of Cachà, the hardest of hard woods, the house is home to 17,000 books, nestled beautifully in their timber homes. A humble raised walkway links the pavilions. For all the timber pyrotechnics of the roof structure and the irregularity of its shape, Casa Kiké is a calm, comfortable and ultimately exquisite place to live, read, dream and simply be.

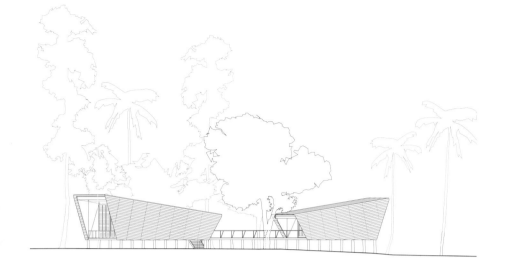

from above to below: elevation of pavilions, work place in library

from left to right, from above to below: bookshelves, master
bedroom, library wall: books and structure become one

from above to below: swimming pool in front of opened façade, main entrance

view from deck towards closed façade

Casa 7A

Villeta, Colombia

Architect: Arquitectura en Estudio + Natalia Heredia
Year of completion: 2014
Gross floor area: 550 m²
Materials used: ocre tinted concrete, timber, natural stone

Roof and patio – two simple elements that define the unique elegance of Casa 7A. Clean and horizontal, the roof frames the landscape and protects from sun and rain, while diluting the limits between inside and outside, between man-made and natural. The patio tames the natural, inviting it to join the architectural in a celebration of unity. The house is masterfully organized through a succession of voids and blocks that live under the roof, open towards the mountains on one side and a series of patios on the other. Ocre tinted in situ concrete and teak dominate the palette of local, natural materials and generate a vivid array of textures, colors and shadows that dance in the sunlight. This understated palace of tranquility is simply stunning.

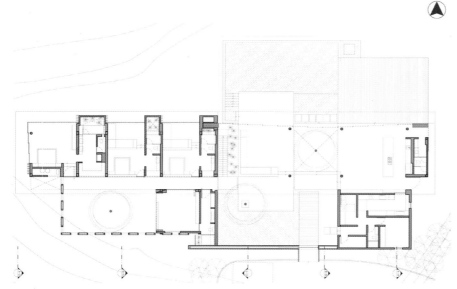

from above to below, from left to right: ground floor plan, swimming pool and patio at night, patio, bathroom

from left to right, from above to below: entrance patio, swimming pool with closed façade, living area

from above to below, from left to right: view of backyard, backyard at night, terrace at night

generous terrace with barbecue

Cachalotes House

La Molina, Lima, Peru

Architect: Gonzalez Moix Architecture
Year of completion: 2009
Gross floor area: 590 m²
Materials used: concrete, wood, stone

Located in an existing condo in La Planicie, Cachalotes House was designed to accommodate a family with one disabled member. All aspects had to be seamlessly integrated without affecting the home's esthetics. The result is a stunning example of perfect functionality and exquisite style. All spaces are neatly embedded in two volumes, the first a single strip and the second containing a double-height social area and terrace expansion. The materials – solid and slatted woods, white façades and glass – speak of warmth and integrity and invite relaxation while the volumes' pure lines, stripped of ornament, respect the parameters of modern, functional design. Large windows provide ventilation and fabulous views across the neighboring golf course.

from above to below, from left to right: double-height living
area, main bathroom, hallway

from left to right, from above to below: living area with view towards dining area, outdoor living area, floor plans and section

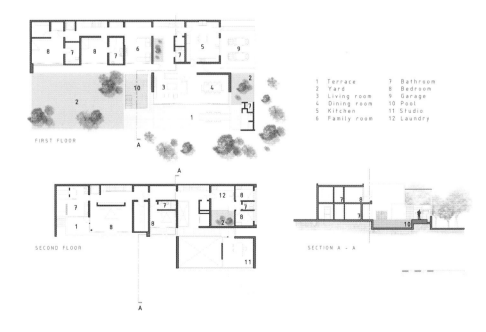

FIRST FLOOR

SECOND FLOOR

SECTION A - A

1	Terrace	7	Bathroom
2	Yard	8	Bedroom
3	Living room	9	Garage
4	Dining room	10	Pool
5	Kitchen	11	Studio
6	Family room	12	Laundry

from above to below, from left to right: main façade opens up,
view towards indoor living area from the side, terrace at night

pool on terrace

Casa Seta

Lima, Peru

Architect: Martín Dulanto Sangalli
Year of completion: 2012
Gross floor area: 156 m²
Materials used: exposed concrete, wood, white painted walls, Talamolle stone, porcelain tiles

This striking house was conceived as a large white box which was excavated to generate habitable spaces. The result is a fabulous manifestation of modern esthetics in harmony with tropical living. The social area located on the ground floor comprises one large space that perfectly integrates its diverse uses – living and dining areas, kitchen and terrace – and blends seamlessly with the exterior gardens. The inventive addition of a sliding door allows the bedrooms on the same level the privacy they require. Vegetation dispersed through the interior perfects the relationship between man-made and natural elements, aided by the rustic quality of the materials chosen. Indeed, this stunningly designed home is the ideal space to enjoy nature and remain in comfort.

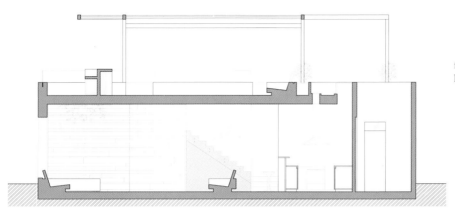

from above to below, from left to right: section, detail corner with living area and terrace, view towards kitchen, kitchen

from left to right, from above to below: living area blurs
boundaries between inside and outside, bedroom, living/
dining area with staircase to terrace

from above to below, from left to right: cube-shaped building
parts with framed views, entrance, patio with pool and tree

view from patio

Taquari House

Brasilia, Brazil

Architect: Ney Lima
Year of completion: 2013
Gross floor area: 380 m²
Materials used: concrete, ceramic coating

To build a home while preserving a tree-studded savanna: this was the dream of the clients for Taquari House. An exquisite U-shaped two-story house was the result – and how stunning it is! An old tree forms a unique centerpiece and contrasts beautifully with the rustic ceramic coating of the facades, reminiscent of traditional adobe houses in the Brazilian state of Goiás. A corten steel entrance door complements the cement and harmonizes with the external coating. Cool whites and vibrant reds are juxtaposed in a celebration of life and color, while circular and rectangular windows offer new perspectives on the natural environment. Ingenuity and style combine to create a truly enviable dwelling.

from above to below, from left to right: longitudinal section, detail entrance door, detail patio with old tree, view through window from patio

from left to right, from above to below: concrete frames
around entrance door and windows, patio, view inside from
patio

from left to right: living area with a view, living area with view
towards dining area and terrace

double-height living area

AMB House

Guarujá, São Paulo, Brazil

Architect: Bernardes+Jacobsen
Arquitetura
Year of completion: 2011
Gross floor area: 810 m²
Materials used: steel structure,
wood

Situated on the São Paulo coast in the middle of the Atlantic Forest, AMB House perfectly juxtaposes respect for nature with bold, modern design. The standard residential layout is reversed, with social areas on the middle floor and bedrooms on the lower, taking advantage of the privacy offered by trees at that level. A hall at the entrance serves as a stunning mezzanine overlooking the double-height, 6-meter-high living room boasting wooden framed windows with a view of the swimming pool and forest. Large glass panels on every floor invite visual contact with the region's magnificent natural landscape. Beautiful shutters made from Cumarú wood and bamboo plants sprouting from the floor perfect this wonderful residence.

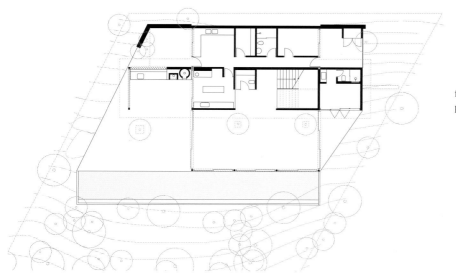

from above to below, from left to right: first floor plan, detail pool, pool with treetops, detail terrace

from left to right, from above to below: barbecue area, terrace
with view towards the sea, view towards house

from above to below, from left to right: master bedroom, staircase, bathroom

from left to right, from above to below: social area with small terrace, upper level terrace, entrance area, cross section

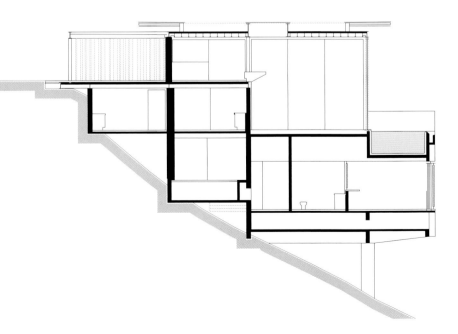

from above to below, from left to right: covered swimming pool,
exterior view from below, exterior side view

view from garden with swimming pool

Bosque da Ribeira Residence

Nova Lima, Brazil

Architect: Anastasia Arquitetos
Year of completion: 2013
Gross floor area: 650 m²
Materials used: steel structure,
wood

Blending beautifully with the adjacent forest, Bosque da Ribeira Residence is a dwelling at one with nature. Standing at the visual interface between environmental reserve and residential area, between nature and mankind, this splendid yet understated structure celebrates the best of both worlds and unites them. The terrace and swimming pool are focused on the landscape, with privacy preserved by the slope, while the building's staggered design skillfully links the residences above with the forest below. A balcony provides esthetic interest and prevents harsh, direct sunlight entering the home. Instead, the interior is bathed in soft, warm rays. Warm woods and natural shades create a calming, welcoming atmosphere that's impossible to resist.

from above to below, from left to right: double-height living
area, living area opens to garden, skylights

from left to right, from above to below: skylit staircase, lounge on upper floor, view down to living area, cross section

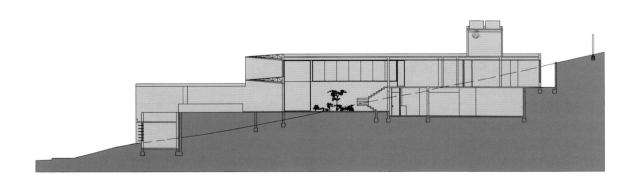

exterior view from garden

living area opens to terrace with pool

Lee House

Porto Feliz, São Paulo, Brazil

Architect: studio mk27 –
Marcio Kogan + Eduardo
Glycerio
Interior designer: studio
mk27 –
Diana Radomysler
Landscape designer: Gil Fialho
Year of completion: 2012
Gross floor area: 900 m²
Materials used: concrete,
wood, glass

Interior and exterior meet in perfect harmony at Lee House. Organized into one single-story volume, every room opens onto the garden with its manicured lawn and lush foliage. Cross-ventilation lowers the internal temperature and wooden muxarabis panels protect the interior from the harsh tropical sun of São Paulo. Divided into two wooden boxes, the living spaces are simply yet

ingeniously planned. The house is clad in stunning white mortar, while beautiful stones encircle the internal patio of the spa. A limited palette of colors and materials, combined with simplicity of design, generates a remarkable and all-embracing minimalist atmosphere that entices and beguiles.

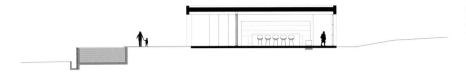

from above to below, from left to right: cross section, glazed hallway, lush foliage in front of the house, exterior detail from the front

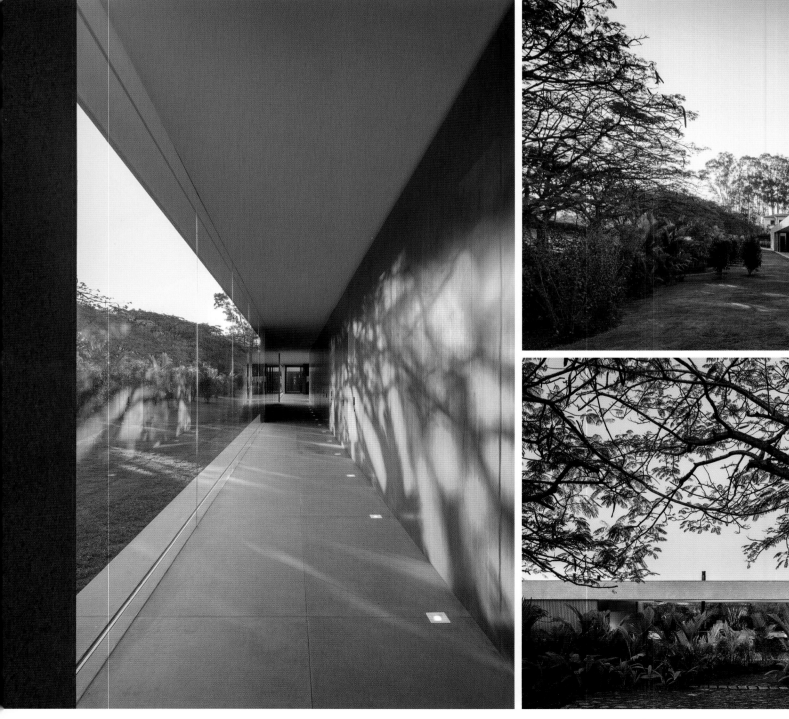

from above to below: living area with bar, open living area
with view towards kitchen and dining area

from above to below, from left to right: master bedroom, bathroom, sauna

from left to right, from above to below: hot tub, terrace, wood and concrete are dominating materials, floor plan

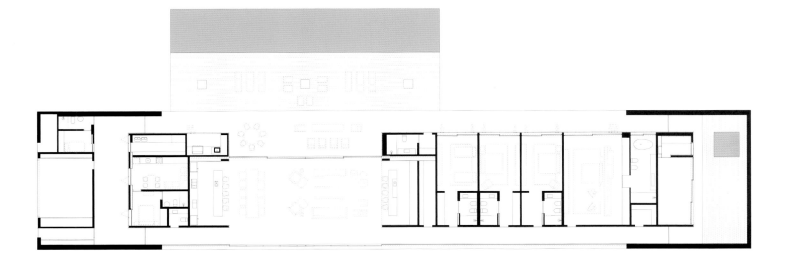

from above to below, from left to right: backyard surrounded by
lush vegetation, swimming pool, main hall

entrance area

Tempo House
Rio de Janeiro, Brazil

Architect: Gisele Taranto Arquitetura
Year of completion: 2011
Gross floor area: 1,500 m²
Materials used: corten steel, peroba do campo wood, Baiteg blue limestone, dark brown aluminum frames

Situated on an extraordinary site bursting with exotic trees and plants in one of the most charming neighborhoods in Rio de Janeiro, this colonial-style house has been completely refurbished in spectacular style. Incorporating a laundry, garage, swimming pool and home theater, it is truly a dream home. Large, clean design spaces and the integration of indoor and outdoor areas generate a wonderful sense of openness and freedom. Sunlight shining through a beautiful glass ceiling bathes a corten steel stairway with light so it appears to be floating in the air. The interior palette of white walls, Baiteg Blue limestone and peroba do campo wood creates an atmosphere of simplicity and unity.

from above to below: ground floor plan, master bedroom, sauna and spa

from left to right, from above to below: dining area, study
room, living area opening to the backyard

from above to below: living area with view towards garden, pool
with panel designed by Athos Bulcão

garden façade of main building

House 7x37

São Paulo, Brazil

Architect: CR2 Architecture
Year of completion: 2013
Gross floor area: 259 m²
Materials used: metallic structure

Compact yet spacious, urban yet rural – this home by CR2 Architecture achieves the impossible! Built as a leisure house for a São Paulo family, less than a kilometer from their everyday apartment, House 7x37 offers the perfect weekend getaway without the travel. Flexible spaces offer limitless possibilities for leisure activities – from barbeques and swimming to sunbathing. The simple garden, together with an eye-catching artistic panel designed by Athos Bulcão Foundation, ingeniously connects all of the ground floor social areas. A beautiful wooden pergola extends from the upper-floor rooms and overlooks the garden. Constructed in just eight months, this home is a superb feat of design and engineering.

from above to below, from left to right: ground floor plan, walk-way along the house towards garden, street façade, walkway along the house

from above to below: living area, dining area and kitchen

from above to below, from left to right: a block of concrete and aluminum rises in the rich vegetation, aluminum façade opens up, opened corner at night

social areas on ground floor can be opened towards the garden

Cube House

São Paulo, Brazil

Architect: studio mk27 – Marcio Kogan + Suzana Glogowski
Interior designer: studio mk27 – Diana Radomysler
Landscape designer: Isabel Duprat
Year of completion: 2012
Gross floor area: 540 m²
Materials used: concrete, glass, aluminum sheets

A monolithic urban house. A single cubic volume. A lantern. It is impossible to encapsulate the architecture of this deceptively simple home. The pure cube is perforated and ripped at strategic places to generate enticing spaces and openings. Metallic panels in the expansive common area can be opened to reveal the garden outside or closed to give the room privacy and shade. The façades comprise rough concrete, expertly shaped using a handcrafted wooden mold, and metallic panels, their color perfectly echoing the adjacent concrete. A specially designed ceramic tile floor forms a continuous fabric in the common area. At night, Casa Cubo becomes a lantern. The dense volume of concrete is muted, giving way to warm rays of internal light.

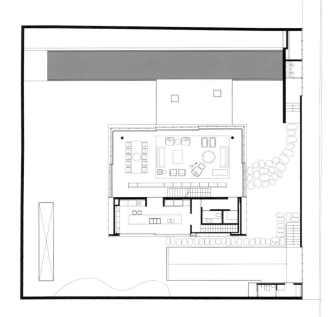

from above to below, from left to right: ground floor plan, pool and deck, view from pool, façade glows like a lantern at night

from above to below: living area, openend dining area at night

from above to below: view from rooftop terrace, master
bedroom

from left to right, from above to below: staircase, home office on second floor, living area with view towards dining area at night, longitudinal section

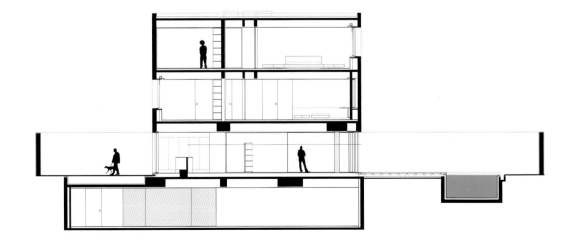

from above to below, from left to right: front façade, view from
the side, detail greened wall

view of balcony and pool

PV House

Itu, São Paulo, Brazil

Architect: Sérgio Sampaio Arquitetura + Planejamento
Year of completion: 2013
Gross floor area: 890 m²
Materials used: metal, concrete, wood, glass

Set on a hillside and dominating the surrounding area with its bold lines, this house truly sets the standard for tropical design. Cleverly subdivided into three blocks, the structure blends functionality with radical esthetics. Services are located downstairs with a terrace for social and leisure activities on the intermediate floor and a suspended pavilion on the second story housing the private

areas. Indoor and outdoor landscapes are integrated in an architectural celebration of natural and human design. Unnecessary beams and pillars are removed to open up a vista of the lagoon in front of the house. Reflecting pool, roof garden and cross ventilation assist in thermal comfort while the rain and wastewater reuse system reduces water consumption.

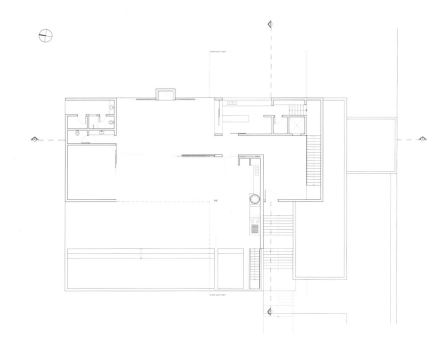

from above to below, from left to right: ground floor plan, detail
pool, outdoor living area, kitchen

from left to right, from above to below: living area, dining
table, deck at dusk

lot in downtown São Paulo

cooling garden area with pool and plants

Weekend House

São Paulo, Brazil

Architect: spbr arquitetos
Year of completion: 2013
Gross floor area: 183 m²
Materials used: concrete, wood, glass

This weekend house in downtown São Paulo is an inspired idea! The residents of that city spend much of their week and weekend stuck in traffic jams, so why not stay in the city for the ideal hassle-free retreat? A garden, solarium and rooftop swimming pool comprise the program's key elements, the most desirable spaces for rest and relaxation. The lack of construction on the ground level enables the greatest possible garden ratio, maximizing the site's potential perfectly. The bedroom, small caretaker's apartment and a space to cook and receive friends happily take second place to the recreation zones. Glass, concrete and warm woods generate a naturally welcoming ambience that offers a welcome retreat from hectic city life.

from above to below, from left to right: pool and deck on
ground floor, kitchen and dining area on ground floor, outdoor
dining area

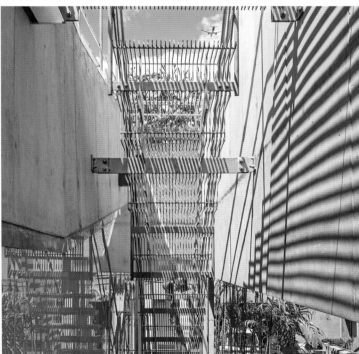

from left to right, from above to below: view from upper floor, rooftop swimming pool, staircase, longitudinal section

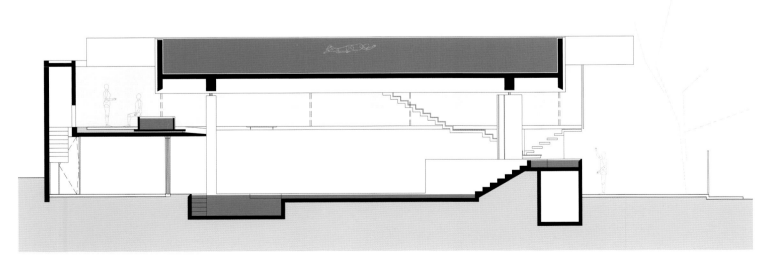

from above to below, from left to right: living area on ground
floor, view towards dining area, garden with swimming pool

from above to below, from left to right: dining area with concrete table, tiled wall, entrance area

DM House

São Paulo, Brazil

Architect: Studio Guilherme Torres
Year of completion: 2012
Gross floor area: 350 m²
Materials used: acrylic paint, wood, tiles, polymer cement (flooring)

Initially an interior design job, the project soon expanded and the original 1970s residence was transformed into a spacious and gorgeously illuminated dwelling. Open to bold ideas, the homeowner welcomed the architect's suggestion of vibrant and colorful decoration. A large multicolor lacquer cabinet was the starting point for the whole project, traversing the rooms, organizing the circulation and giving the house a unique atmosphere. The usage of space is revolutionary, the architect locating the children's bedrooms and games rooms on the ground floor and a living and kitchen area in the basement. A beautiful mosaic tile wall perfectly contrasts the concrete dining-room table. DM House surely sets a new standard in radical contemporary design.

from above to below, from left to right: TV room on upper
floor with colored cabinet wall, reading zone, kitchen

from left to right, from above to below: staircase, red children's room, blue-green children's room, upper floor plan

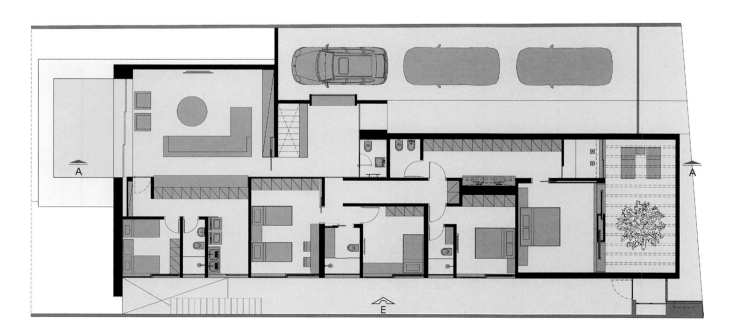

from above to below, from left to right: double-height living area,
U-shaped building parts, staircase

view from the street

Casa Bacopari

Alto de Pinheiros, São Paulo, Brazil

Architect: UNA Arquitetos
Year of completion: 2012
Gross floor area: 504 m²
Materials used: concrete, steel, wood

Located in a neighborhood with abundant afforestation, Casa Bacopari is the perfect architectural counterpart to its natural surroundings. The large garden permeates the house providing continuity with the existing vegetation and creating a new relationship between the man-made and natural landscapes. Transparent glass and open spaces contrast with concrete walls and steel supports, generating a balanced and harmonious whole. The succession of open and closed spaces, produced by glass façades, water tanks and dark panels, generate series of reflections and transparencies diluting the boundaries between inside and outside. This blissful sanctuary is the manifestation of perfect design, combining simple luxury and unity with nature.

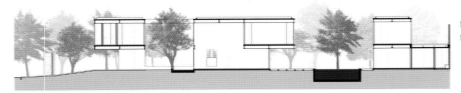

from above to below, from left to right: longitudinal section, patio from above, patio, garden

from left to right, from above to below: upper floor, living area
on ground floor, living area with view towards dining area
and patio

from above to below: living area on ground floor, detail window

living area extends outdoor

Patio House

São Paulo, Brazil

Architect: AR Architects
Year of completion: 2012
Gross floor area: 420 m²
Materials used: concrete, white walls, wooden floors

Inspired by Gordon Matta-Clark's building cuts and James Turrell's skyscapes, Patio House stands as a unique and arresting structure in the landscape. An existing construction was maintained and newly interpreted as a solid to be excavated, its negative spaces subverting the old spatial syntax. The result is a compelling monument to contemporary design perfectly harmonizing with nature. Plants and trees invade the internal spaces and peer in at windows, drawing the eye to their lush foliage. Internal patios function as 'decompression areas' between uses and blur conventional boundaries between interior and exterior. An old garage becomes a vibrant living space while a stunning suspended patio dominates the middle level. Tropical living is a pleasure in this serene space.

from above to below, from left to right: master bedroom, detail façade, garden

from left to right, from above to below: garden, terrace on upper floor, patio with tree, conceptual diagram

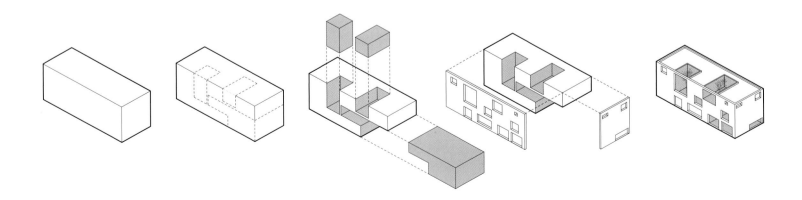

from above to below: indoor dining and living area, view from the street

deck with pool

AN House

Maringá, Paraná, Brazil

Architect: Studio Guilherme Torres
Year of completion: 2013
Gross floor area: 800 m²
Materials used: wood, Carrara marble, cement

Situated in a condominium in Paraná, Brazil, AN House is a remarkable and highly sophisticated piece of tropical architecture. Large open spans, cross-flow and wooden "brise soleils" work together to mitigate the effects of the hot climate. Exposed concrete, white brickwork and Cumaru wood combine in simple esthetic harmony to please the eye and inspire the mind. Coated with stones and embellished with tropical plants, the exterior walls manifest the perfect relationship between human and natural design. A special irrigation system ensures that this rather unusual vertical garden remains lush and verdant. Style and elegance, innovation and boldness – AN House truly deserves a place in the fascinating story of tropical design.

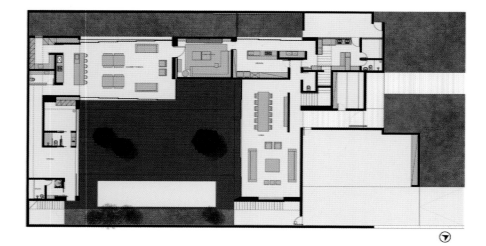

from above to below, from left to right: ground floor plan, living area, living area opens towards garden, view towards dining area

from left to right, from above to below: outdoor dining area
and kitchen, hallway, outdoor dining table

from above to below: view from garden, view from the street

family room

L House

Buenos Aires, Argentina

Architect: Mathias Klotz /
Edgardo Minond
Year of completion: 2010
Gross floor area: 420 m²
Materials used: concrete, glass

This dazzling single-family home is located in Olivos, a beautiful old neighborhood of Buenos Aires, on a rectangular site dotted randomly with trees. The garden is the centerpiece, the modest program paying homage to the natural beauty of the surroundings and inviting contemplative interaction with the exterior. Organized in a series of squares linked by a linear circulation, the interior spaces exude a minimalist esthetic that calms and enthralls. Concrete and travertine, steel and wood generate solidity and establish a fluid and harmonious dialogue between interior and exterior. This really is a triumph of functionality and esthetic perfection.

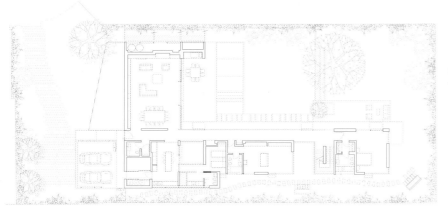

from above to below, from left to right: ground floor plan, garden view, living area, dining area

from above to below: view from pool at night, hallway and
dining area

from above to below: lounge area, garden

outdoor dining area with magnificent view

De Wet 34
Cape Town, South Africa

Architect: SAOTA – Stefan Antoni Olmesdahl Truen Architects
Year of completion: 2012
Gross floor area: 1,057 m²
Materials used: concrete, steel, glass, dark gray shale stone, American redwood, granite

Raw, primal, ancient, timeless, mystical: inspired by these words, SAOTA created this superb dwelling in the heart of Bantry Bay. The modest street façade in dark gray shale stone and sustainable American redwood belies the treasures beyond. Imposing granite stepping-stones lead through a mystic sculpture courtyard lush with fever trees and cycads. Neo Sardo granite floors with a hand-hewn soft edge lend the interior spaces a timeless quality. The astounding views create drama at every turn as you move through the house on an emotional and sensorial journey. Subtly organic décor and locally crafted pieces personalize the simple interior and generate an ambiance of serenity. Comfort and relaxation are never far away in this beautiful home.

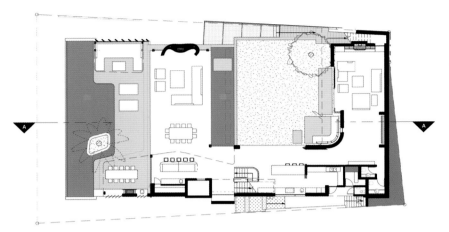

from above to below, from left to right: first floor plan, staircase with skylight, view from entrance, entrance area

from left to right, from above to below: master bedroom,
bathroom, dining area

from above to below, from left to right: terrace with pool,
study, private gallery

from left to right, from above to below: atrium with skylight, lounge at night, garden at night with fireplace, section

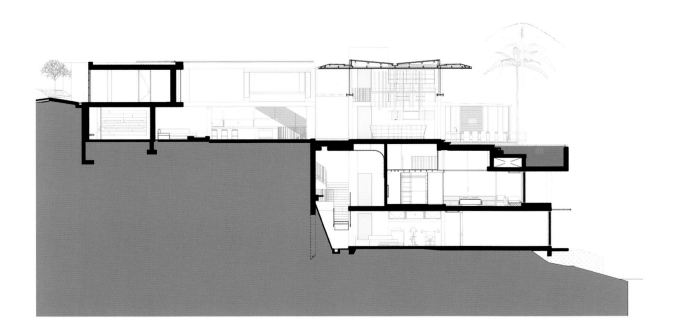

double-height living/lounge area

view from the street

Pentagon
Cape Town, South Africa

Architect: SAOTA –
Stefan Antoni Olmesdahl Truen
Architects
Year of completion: 2011
Gross floor area: 1,624 m²
Materials used: concrete, steel,
glass, aluminum, Rheinzink,
dark gray and white paint, wal-
nut veneer, granite, mirror

A dramatic, triple-volume gallery-like space welcomes the visitor into the residence. The drama unfolds in the living space on the second upper level, which enjoys magnificent 270-degree views. An emotional and sensorial journey through the house provides excitement at every turn, from fabulous views to shifting interior moods. Clean, geometric lines co-exist harmoniously with soft, intimate interior décor, natural and subtly organic. The furniture and lighting are predominantly selected from the OKHA product range, made locally by skilled artisans with locally sourced materials. The bold, dark external color allows the structure to visually recede into the mountainous backdrop, while inviting the curious passerby to take a closer look.

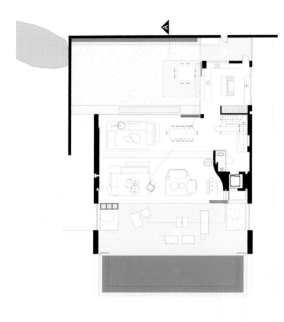

from above to below, from left to right: first floor plan, staircase,
art on upper floor, dining area on first floor

from above to below: lounge with view towards terrace and
sea, interior living area extends seamlessly to the terrace

from above to below, from left to right: living area with view
to terrace, double-height space, lounge area

from above to below: master bedroom above living area, section

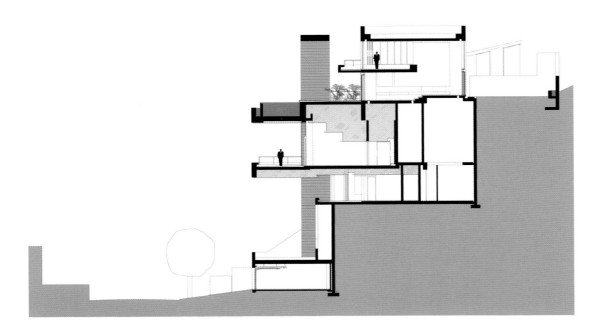

142

from above to below: bedroom featuring furniture made from
organic and locally sourced materials, aerial view of North Island

piazza and main beach

North Island Villas

North Island, Seychelles

Architect: Silvio Rech, Lesley Carstens
Year of completion: 2003
Gross floor area: 2,000,000 m²
Materials used: local wood, gumpoles, copper, brass, sandstone, granite rock

North Island Villas are truly the epitome of luxury tropical living. Developed as a private resort for guests, these 11 beautiful villas perfectly complement the breathtaking scenery with their natural timbers, and seamless merging of interior and exterior. Cool white textiles, glowing lamps and a neutral palette soothe the eye and invite relaxation. The luxury development intends to reintroduce the Sey-chelles' natural flora and fauna, including giant tortoises and certain birds. Offering an all-inclusive and very private holiday experience, with on-call butler service and any menu any venue dining experiences, North Island is the ideal refuge from the stresses of life and the ultimate place to relax amidst stunning natural beauty and high-touch design.

143

from above to below, from left to right: floor plan Presidential Villa, private deck overlooking the beach, Presidential Villa bedroom, lounge area with deck

from above to below: East Beach, sala overlooking palm-
fringed beach

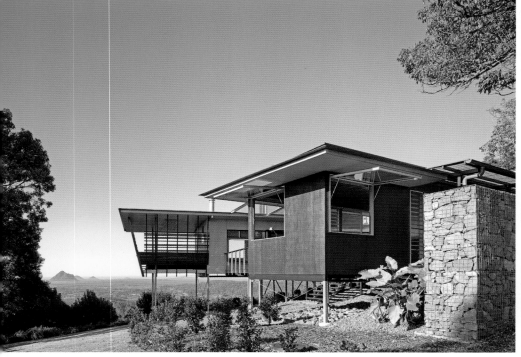

from above to below, from left to right: view from entrance area, house nestled in surroundings, open studio

covered walkway to courtyard

Glass House Mountains House

Maleny, Australia

Architect: Bark Design Architects
Year of completion: 2009
Gross floor area: 509 m²
Materials used: steel, plywood, timber, glass

Engaging with existing topography, orientation, views and vegetation, the spectacular "Glass House Mountain House" balances economy and fine craft. Surfaces, finishes and details exhibit the Japanese concept of "wabi sabi" – the beauty of things imperfect, impermanent and incomplete, allowed to weather and evolve with time. Perched on the edge of a mountain range, the dwell-

ing celebrates the surrounding sky and mountains in its very structure. Translated into a place of glass and stone inextricably connected to its landscape it has qualities of being anchored, robust and earthbound as well as being transparent, light and floating. Who could resist the allure of such bold, yet sophisticated architecture?

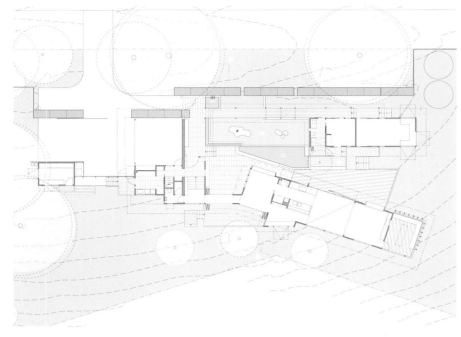

from above to below, from left to right: ground floor plan, double-height entrance area, dining area, patio at dusk

from left to right, from above to below: kitchen with terrace,
view of spectacular landscape, balcony

from above to below, from left to right: lily pond, entrance pod
sweeps gently along the hills, roof is angled to protect from
monsoon

open living area and verandah

Leaf House

Alibaug, Maharashtra, India

Architect: M/s. SJK Architects
Year of completion: 2012
Gross floor area: 650 m²
Materials used: concrete, cement plaster, recycled teakwood, glass, Kotah stone floor

A plot of land in the coastal area of Alibaug was to become a family home, nestled at the base of the hills and removed from the sea. The surrounding hills, trees and gentle breezes provided the inspiration for the form – a series of gently sloping, curving leaves that envelop and shade. Dense concrete and steel were used to generate beamless leaf-shells that retained the simple, natural colors of their materials. Each leaf-shaded pod was created with an eye to the sun and the winds, offering the perfect combination of warmth and welcome breezes. Natural forms encounter man-made constructs at every turn. Yet this encounter generates a wonderfully serene and perfectly natural environment for a family to live in complete comfort.

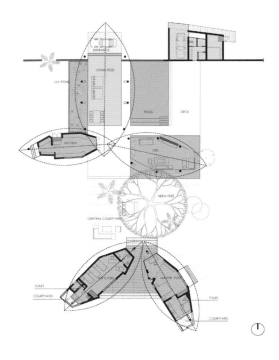

from above to below, from left to right: floor plan, the pods' structures interact, bathroom, courtyard acts as extended living area

from left to right, from above to below: swimming pool,
master bedroom, living area at dusk

153

from above to below, from left to right: double-height library opens to verandah, library, library with bookshelves

from above to below, from left to right: tropical entrance courtyard, old pot in courtyard, collonaded walkway

The Library House

Bangalore, India

Architect: Khosla Associates
Year of completion: 2013
Gross floor area: 1,162 m²
Materials used: yellow Jaiselmer stone, Kotah stone, teakwood, Sadharhalli stone, floral patterned terrazzo tiles, terracotta roofing tiles

Seeking a peaceful oasis from the stresses of life, the clients turned to Khosla Associates who created just that. With space to breathe, a verandah to watch the rain fall and a garden to potter about in, this ecologically sensitive house with abundant natural light and ventilation perfectly combines functionality and beauty. From the road, a modest yet striking colonnaded Mangalore tiled covered walkway with wooden columns traverses a tropical courtyard replete with a fishpond, yellow ochre walls, and an ancestral swing. Sliding doors and open-plan layouts create a grand and seamless living space that unites old and new, global and Indian in the inspired choice of colonial tile, teakwood and stunning pieces by Italian brands Moroso and Emu.

from above to below, from left to right: garden and verandah,
view from garden towards swimming pool with first floor
bedrooms hovering over, swimming pool

from left to right, from above to below: dining area, entrance foyer with art installations, double-height foyer, ground floor plan

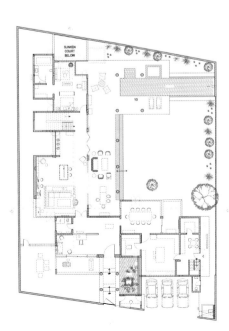

from above to below, from left to right: double-height living area opens to deck and garden, pool deck and dining area, entrance area

exterior view reflecting in the pond

Monsoon Retreat

Khandala, Maharashtra, India

Architect: Abraham John
Architects
Year of completion: 2013
Gross floor area: 777 m²
Materials used: glass, engi-
neered wood, sandstone

Privacy and openness – these apparently contradictory ideas are united in harmony at Monsoon Retreat. Refuge from the world can be sought and found at the tranquil poolside and in the interior spaces veiled by foliage from prying eyes. Every room opens up to a private outdoor space, one's very own natural haven. Indoor/outdoor boundaries blur and disappear. The carefully chosen, limited palette of materials ensures consistency in design, minimizes maintenance and encourages sustainability by using 'green' materials that accentuate warmth and transparency, whilst aging beautifully. Not just esthetically arresting, the sloping roofs are designed to withstand extreme rainfall. This really is the perfect 'Monsoon Retreat'.

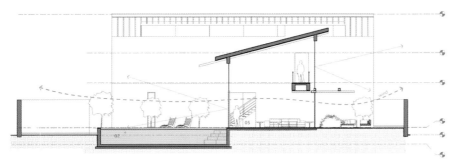

from above to below, from left to right: section, pool with rustic stone wall at night, indoor garden at staircase, staircase with double-height windows

from left to right, from above to below: dining area seen from above through skylight in front of master bedroom, dining area at night, master bedroom with terrace

from above to below: pool scenery seen from upper deck, view from the street

from above to below, from left to right: pools, view from indoor living area, view from upper deck at night

Villa Paya-Paya

Seminyak, Bali, Indonesia

Architect: Aboday Architect
Year of completion: 2010
Gross floor area: 450 m²
Materials used: concrete, wood, glass

Located in Seminyah, a bustling residential area in the heart of Bali, Villa Paya-Paya is a sublime holiday residence. The magical destination of Bali is sought after by holidaymakers around the globe, yet this site began as a humble pig farm and papaya plantation. Now it is home to a modest yet stylish villa that juxtaposes traditional design with contemporary innovation. The simple concrete white box structure departs from typical Balinese architecture with sloping coconut-leaf roofs, yet a closer look reveals a beautiful traditional sloping wooden roof in the master bedroom pavilion. Water envelops the structure, soothing and cooling by its presence. The effect is mesmerizing – the villa appears to float atop a tranquil pool of water.

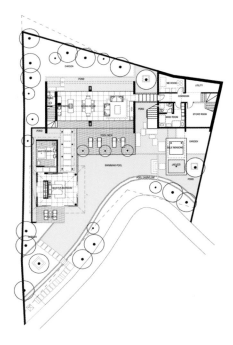

from above to below, from left to right: ground floor plan, night view, detail water feature

from left to right, from above to below: view from above,
hallway, detail pool

from above to below: dining area, exterior view from the street

living area, opening to pool deck

Villa Pecatu

Bali, Indonesia

Architect: Wahana Architects
Year of completion: 2013
Gross floor area: 900 m²
Materials used: concrete structure, brick, various kinds of wood and stone

Located on the reserved hilly limestone landscape of Pecatu, a beach resort in the southern peninsula of Bali, Villa Pecatu is a striking 900-square-meter private villa boasting five bedrooms and recreational facilities. The design language is simple yet sophisticated. Two primary buildings separate public and private spaces, connected with a semi-outdoor bridge – a humble composition that respects the contours of the site and defers to the vast panorama of its surroundings. The living and dining areas in the first building are designed as openly as possible, gesturing towards the outdoor pool area and exotic landscape, while the rooms upstairs enjoy magnificent sea views. Boldly exposed natural stone creates an exquisite architectural experience.

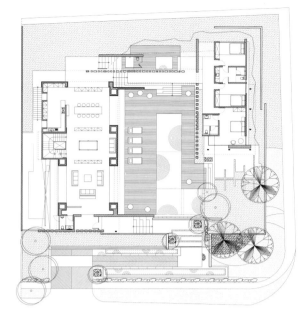

from above to below, from left to right: ground floor plan, covered outdoor bridge, view towards the sea, view from upper floor

from left to right, from above to below: master bedroom,
jacuzzi nestled in natural surroundings, swimming pool

from above to below: interior living area, entrance deck

from above to below, from left to right: living area on mezzanine floor, ground floor living area, lounge in master bedroom

Lalaland Residence

Canggu, Bali, Indonesia

Architect: Word of Mouth
Year of completion: 2008
Gross floor area: 560 m²
Materials used: recycled teakwood (structure), polished concrete (floor)

Lalaland is the affectionately named and highly sophisticated home of architect Valentina Audrito and her family, located in Canggu, Bali. A refurbishment of an existing residence done originally by Mauro Tomasi, the villa has been adapted to suit the needs of its new inhabitants, with the introduction of mezzanine spaces to enhance comfort and introduce a sense of privacy, whilst retaining the beautiful old teak structures and timber flooring. The interior furnishings are best described as eclectic, all of which sit in comfortable contrast to the traditional joglo structure and materiality. The space and its furnishing exhibit a liberating refusal to be restricted to any particular style, and manifest perfectly the evolving expression of its inhabitants and the way they choose to live.

171

from above to below, from left to right: pool deck, children's room, kitchen with dining area

from left to right, from above to below: walk-in closet, detail living room, master bathroom, ground floor plan

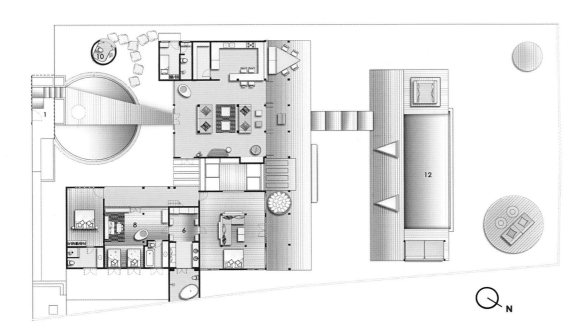

from above to below, from left to right: view towards living area,
front façade, inner garden with view through living area

main entrance area

Diminished House

Cipete, Jakarta, Indonesia

Architect: Wahana Architects
Year of completion: 2011
Gross floor area: 550 m²
Materials used: concrete structure, brick, various kinds of wood and stone

Diminshed House is the stunning result of a renovation project. Since fewer rooms were required in the renovated structure, the size of the house was simply reduced, generating the unique possibility for each room to have an outdoor space. The primary structure was preserved along with the magnificent trees at the front and back, later playing their role in creating the green scenery enjoyed from the family room and master bedroom. Open and transparent, the family room is the heart of the house and welcomes with its warmth. Local materials such as andesite stones and bengkirai woods combined with teak waste are used as interior and exterior elements, generating an exquisite architectural impression of interconnected indoor and outdoor space.

from above to below, from left to right: floor plan, swimming pool, study room from outside, interior view study room

from above to below: hallway extends outdoors through the
inner garden, master bedroom

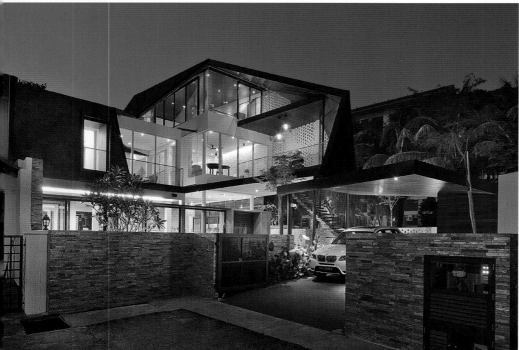

from above to below, from left to right: the roof bends and folds around the house, entrance at night, balconies on upper floors

front façade

Re-wrapped House

Singapore, Singapore

Architect: A D Lab
Year of completion: 2012
Gross floor area: 530 m²
Materials used: painted brick,
wood, marble

A masterful piece of architectural design, this stunning semi-detached house in Singapore is truly one of a kind. Working on an existing 1970s house, the designers studied the structure as one would study a living organism, creating a space invigorated with new life and in harmony with its built and tropical surroundings. A gap between the old and new structures was an inspired decision, allowing light and air to flow freely through the house. Organically organized painted brick forms a fabulous multi-functional "breathing" wall. Creating beautiful patterns of light across the inner surfaces of the dwelling, the wall generates a calm and peaceful atmosphere where space is in harmony with history, climate and the natural elements.

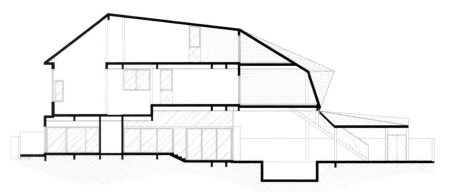

from above to below, from left to right: section, staircase, swimming pool and terrace, living area

from left to right, from above to below: bathroom, study room,
gap between old and new structure – living and dining area

from above to below: living area with view towards greened wall, front façade at night

dining area and terrace

Tan's Garden Villa

Singapore, Singapore

Architect: Aamer Architects
Year of completion: 2012
Gross floor area: 342 m²
Materials used: timber, marble, granite

In 2001, Aamer Architects was commissioned to design two houses in the same street. They did such a good job, winning the prestigious Singapore Institute of Architects' Design Award, that they were asked back ten years later to design a new house. The result is a gorgeous complement to the existing dwellings. Timber, marble and granite dominate, the strong textures and tones balancing the soft foliage of the vertically stacked gardens. Creepers hug the vertical timber trellises and rise towards the sky in a celebration of natural and human design. A rooftop swimming pool offers tranquil views and welcome relief from the scorching sun. Birds and butterflies are attracted by the lush flora bringing life and color to this exquisite home.

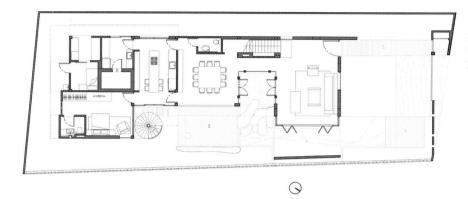

from above to below, from left to right: ground floor plan, green terrace with spiral staircase to upper floors, terrace with fish pond, master bathroom

from left to right, from above to below: glass bottom pool
skylight over courtyard, exterior side view with swimming
pool, rooftop swimming pool

from above to below, from left to right: living area by the pool,
bridge verandah, view from garden

view from driveway

David's B & W

Singapore, Singapore

Architect: Aamer Architects
Year of completion: 2012
Gross floor area: 882 m²
Materials used: tropical hardwood, bamboo, marble, timber

One man's dream has become reality, thanks to the remarkable design skills of Aamer Architects. This traditional 'black & white' colonial-style home is the manifestation of what was for so long an unfulfilled wish. The striking structure is neatly split into two blocks linked with an elegant verandah bridge above the impressive swimming pool. Large covered terraces extend the interior spaces to the poolside areas, reviving the charming colonial lifestyle of a bygone era. Generous gardens boasting beautiful, lush flora perfectly complement the tropical living environment. Guests are welcomed in the 'out-house', where even the most discerning visitor will be enchanted by the luxurious accommodation.

from above to below, from left to right: master block, bridges
and verandahs, verandah in front of children's bedrooms

from left to right, from above to below: basement courtyard, home cinema in the basement, guest villa with koi pond, design sketch

from above to below: courtyard at night, garden at night

from above to below, from left to right: detail wing, study room, tropical greenery surrounds the house

Winged House

Singapore, Singapore

Architect: K2LD Architects
Year of completion: 2012
Gross floor area: 800 m²
Materials used: rustic yellow granite, timber, teak, chengai

A family residence situated on a unique triangular plot, the Winged House frames the site with two unusual and prominent forms – trapeziums. Opening majestically towards the main view, these forms astound the eye and beguile the senses, carving out and framing a middle garden for private gatherings. Drawing on a deep understanding of traditional Malay architecture, the designers created a structure that pays homage to that heritage while breaking new ground in contemporary design. The main entrance foyer is flanked with two natural split granite walls – a perfect complement to the lightness of the roofs and vertical timber lines. This desirable abode sits snugly in a serene 'winged' embrace of the site and dwelling within.

from above to below: covered terrace, courtyard

from left to right, from above to below: floating roof, staircase, living area, ground floor plan

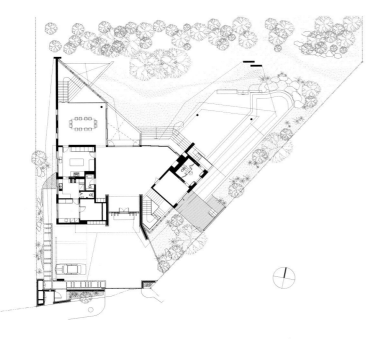

from above to below, from left to right: exterior view from the
street, detail façade, entrance area

water feature in front of the house

Far Sight House

Singapore, Singapore

Architect: Wallflower
Architecture + Design
Year of completion: 2013
Gross floor area: 463 m²
Materials used: travertine,
balau, teakwood, granite, alumi-
num screens

Resting on high ground and with wonderful views overlooking green and affluent residential areas, Far Sight
House is a stylish example of contemporary design.
A multi-layered façade of operable glass doors and
windows, vertical timber louvers, horizontal aluminum
sunscreens and blinds generate a multitude of esthetic
and textured impressions and enable the owner to control
sunlight, breezes and views. Filtered light bathes the internal spaces, leaving no corner in darkness nor any spot too
bright. An attic terrace with 'million-dollar views' acts as a
literal 'light-house', gathering the sun's rays and offering a
spectacular vista. This home is the perfect place to relax,
unwind and rediscover harmony with nature.

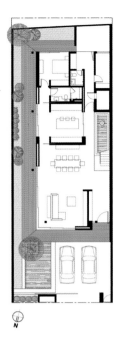

from above to below, from left to right: ground floor plan, hallway with staircase, study with a view, living area

from left to right, from above to below: dining area on ground
floor, kitchen, terrace overlooking the area

from above to below, from left to right: view of the ocean from
the pool deck, general view, view across the sea from below

from above to below, from left to right: view inside, view outside through the open shutters, entrance area

Villa Vista

Weligama, Sri Lanka

Architect: Shigeru Ban
Architects
Year of completion: 2010
Gross floor area: 825 m²
Materials used: reinforced
concrete, steel, timber, coconut
leaves, teak wood

After designing and building post-tsunami houses in Sri Lanka, Shigeru Ban was commissioned for a rather different project. Villa Vista, located on a stunning hilltop site facing the ocean, is home to the owner of a local tire company. As its name suggests, this house is all about the views. The first reveals the ocean framed perpendicularly as seen from the jungle in the valley, while the second provides a horizontal ocean view and the third a cliff glowing red in the evening sunset. Whatever your taste, there's a vista to astound and seduce! Light cement boards and woven coconut leaves cover the roof, merging the structure with its natural surroundings. Teak ceilings are woven in a large wickerwork pattern that is echoed through the interior.

from above to below, from left to right: dining area and terrace, pool deck framing the view of the ocean, interior view

from left to right, from above to below: window framing the view, pool deck, wood dominates the interior, upper floor plan

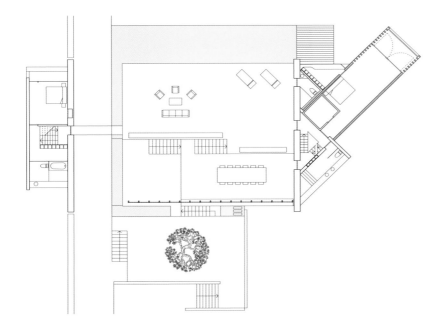

from above to below: main entrance, exterior side view

master bedroom with bathroom

Wonderwall House

Chiangmai, Thailand

Architect: SO (Situation based Operation) – Narong Othavorn
Year of completion: 2012
Gross floor area: 600 m²
Materials used: concrete, brick

Simplicity, functionality and a good dose of style – Wonderwall House is like nothing you've seen before! Comprising a large open-plan living space that merges seamlessly with the perfectly designed outdoor spaces, this residence invites total relaxation. The architects daringly chose a brick wall as the central feature and it works supremely well. Cutting through the existing landform within the plot to create the sequential scenes, it exposes unexpected spaces and functions and controls the visibility of each space. A square terrace on an upper level doubles as a cinema – ideal for those lazy summer evenings. Red clay bricks, timber decking and exposed concrete – a simple palette for a simple, yet inspired tropical home.

from above to below, from left to right: section, outdoor cinema court, entrance to common area, staircase

from above to below: master bedroom with private pool,
common area

from above to below, from left to right: sliding panel on terrace, exterior side view, side view

barbecue roof deck

Prime Nature Residence

Bangplee, Samutprakarn, Thailand

Architect: Department of Architecture
Year of completion: 2011
Gross floor area: 480 m²
Materials used: concrete, wooden floor, metal lattice screens, sheer canvas panels

Situated at a busy intersection in a residential estate that forbids fences, the site posed an immediate problem for the architects. The solution is undoubtedly inspired! A series of small vertical planes is projected onto a grid at varying distances from the house, cleverly blocking out intruding views and ventilating the outdoor area. Lattice panels and swaying trees cast beautifully delicate shadow patterns on the terrace floor and building elevations. Canvas planes become the screen for black and white movie animations generated by the dramatic moving shadows of passing car headlights. Filled with playful and imaginative shadow and reflection, the house is a unique and dazzling dwelling.

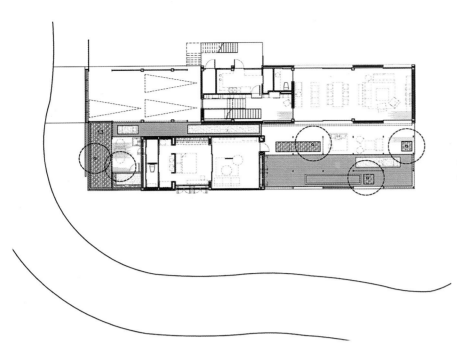

from above to below, from left to right: ground floor plan, living
area continues outdoors, living area, kitchen

from left to right, from above to below: vertical panes frame
the terrace, jacuzzi in master bedroom, lush vegetation around
the house

from above to below, from left to right: master bedroom, living area, greened façade

from above to below, from left to right: detail façade, entrance area, view from the street

Stacking Green

Ho Chi Minh City, Vietnam

Architect: Vo Trong Nghia
Architects
Year of completion: 2011
Gross floor area: 215 m²
Materials used: concrete,
granite, terazzo, oak wood

Stacking Green embodies a challenge to the increasingly uniform esthetic of developing Asian cities that are losing their regional characteristics under the influence of furious urban sprawl and commercialization. Greenery is disappearing and quality of life is falling. Yet plants and flowers have always been welcomed in Ho Chi Minh City and this striking design has ingeniously translated this custom into architecture. The façade is composed of planters that contribute not only esthetically but also improve internal temperatures, privacy and security. Automatic irrigation pipes inside the planters enable watering, for which rainwater is collected and pumped. This home is truly a unique and inspirational chapter in the history of residential design.

from above to below, from left to right: master bathroom,
rooftop terrace, staircase

from above to below, from left to right: kitchen seen from living area, skylight, hallway, design sketch section

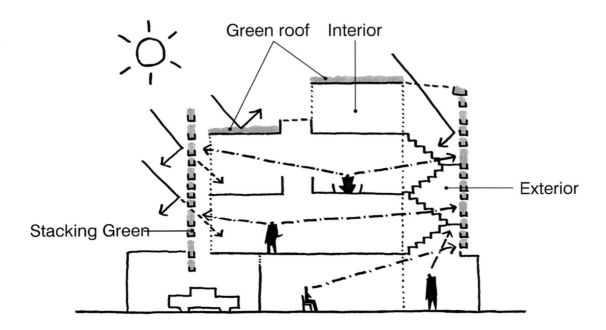

from above to below: beach façade, general view from the beach

swimming pool extends visually to the sea

Oceanique Villas

Mui Ne, Vietnam

Architect: MM++ Architects
Year of completion: 2014
Gross floor area: 1,014 m²
Materials used: concrete, solid timber, aluminum

The idyllic holiday destination of Mui Ne on Vietnam's south east coast is now home to a new real estate development. To take advantage of the stunning views, the designers conceived a trapezoidal structure of semi-detached villas, each with a private swimming pool and raised 1.8 meters from beach level to maintain perfect privacy and improve the view even more. The materials are simple and the design minimalist, paying homage to the awesome sights offered by the natural environment. Large aluminum framed windows on the beach façade and timber louvers at the back maintain the desired simplicity. These villas really are the perfect place in which to dream and rediscover harmony with nature.

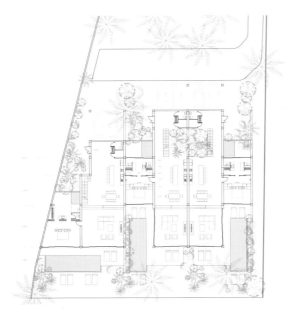

from above to below, from left to right: ground floor plan villas, outdoor jacuzzi, master bedroom, view at night

from left to right, from above to below: covered patio, kitchen
area, staircase with water feature

from above to below, from left to right: view from inner courtyard, view from the street, entrance area

rusk mat room

Viet Pavilion

Ninh Binh, Vietnam

Architect: Landmak Architecture, JSC
Year of completion: 2013
Gross floor area: 423 m²
Materials used: local stone, brick

Eminently local, thoroughly urban, perfectly traditional yet utterly modern – Viet Pavilion is a remarkable architectural achievement. The house is located in Vietnam's ancient capital, a bustling urban space replete with complex and diverse architectural styles. A series of stone walls structure the magnificent residence and combine to create contrasting spaces – closed and open, inside and outside, old and new. Natural elements – sun, rain, wind – are free to enter in a perfect symbiosis of nature and mankind. The spaces are inspired by elements of traditional Vietnamese life: a village pagoda and pond and an old brick fireplace, existing only in fading memory for many Vietnamese. Charming and stylish, this home stands as testament to human innovation.

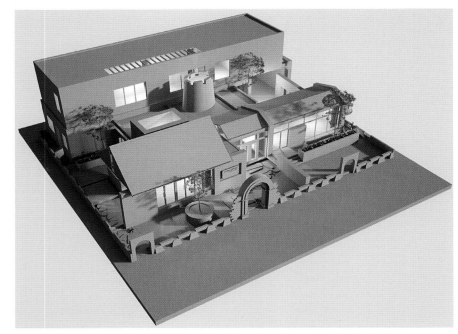

from above to below, from left to right: 3D-model, interior pond,
view from pond, social area

from left to right, from above to below: entrance area, exterior
detail, outdoor social area

from above to below, from left to right: double-height living area,
view from main deck, living area continues outdoor

from above to below, from left to right: house nestled in the forest, kitchen and dining area, deck

Deck House

Bentong, Pahang, Malaysia

Architect: Choo Gim Wah
Year of completion: 2012
Gross floor area: 370 m²
Materials used: steel, glass, aluminum louvers, timber

Located in the lush greenery of the Janda Baik forest in the foothills of Genting Highlands, the Deck House is simple and unassuming yet highly innovative. Despite its unconventional steel and glass look, the house functions perfectly like a traditional tropical house with high ceilings, well-lit interior spaces and excellent ventilation. Large outdoor areas provide the ideal space in which to relax, dream and enjoy the region's magnificent views and fresh air. The extensive use of timber creates an extraordinarily rich and warm texture, contrasting the steel and glass and complementing the warm textures of the neighboring forest. Coziness and comfort, elegance and sophistication combine in perfect unity at the Deck House.

from above to below, from left to right: entrance on upper
floor, master bedroom, decks

from left to right, from above to below: living area from above, staircase, deck looking inside, design sketch elevation

from above to below, from left to right: living area, courtyard,
outdoor dining area

view from the street

Courtyard House

Paranaque City, Philippines

Architect: Atelier Sacha Cotture
Year of completion: 2011
Gross floor area: 460 m²
Materials used: bamboo poles, araal stone, romblon marble, capiz, mahogany

Simple materials and clean lines deliver a sophisticated residence created by Atelier Sacha Cotture. Bamboo façades create a compelling esthetic finish, while also being low cost, sustainable and local. Indeed, bamboo has been used in the Philippines throughout history in the creation of handicrafts, functional items and native architecture. The home's windows, cabinets and beds are hewn out of majestic local mahogany. Imbued with history, this wood represents both an admirable respect for the past and hope for a sustainable future. A pond borders the serene courtyard and boasts an exquisite water feature, enjoyed best from the comfort of the interior living spaces. In this space, worldly cares can be forgotten and dreams indulged.

from above to below, from left to right: ground floor plan, bamboo façade, hallway, courtyard from above

from left to right, from above to below: master bedroom,
dining area, detail staircase

Architects'/Designers' Index

A D Lab Pte Ltd
>> 178

229 Joo Chiat Road, #02-01
Singapore 427489 (Singapore)
T +65.6346.0488
F +65.6346.3488
admin@a-dlab.com
www.a-dlab.com

Aamer Architects – Aamer Taher
>> 182, 186

5 Burn Road, #06-02
Singapore 369972 (Singapore)
T +65.6280.3776
F +65.6280.7743
info@aamertaher.com
www.aamertaher.com

Aboday
>> 162

Jalan Kemang Selatan I/16C
Jakarta Selatan 12730 (Indonesia)
T +62.21.719.3664
F +62.21.719.1430
www.aboday.com

Abraham John Architects
>> 158

31 Green acre, Union Park Road
No. 5
Khar (W), Bombay 400052 (India)
T +91.22.2600.0081
info@abrahamjohnarchitects.com
www.abrahamjohnarchitects.com

Anastasia Arquitetos
>> 78

Rua Orenoco 137, LJ 01 Carmo
CEP 30310-060 Belo Horizonte
(Brazil)
T +55.31.3282.1334
anastasia@anastasiaarquitetos.com.br
www.anastasiaarquitetos.com.br

AR Architects
>> 118

Av. Paulista, n2644 cj 125
01310-300 São Paulo, SP (Brazil)
T +55.11.3663.4465
F +55.11.3663.4465
contato@ar-arquitetos.com.br
www.ar-arquitetos.com.br

Arquitectura en Estudio
>> 56

Calle 80 # 8–85, Of. 301
Bogota (Colombia)
T +57.1.345.4587
contacto@arquitecturaenestudio.com
www.arquitecturaenestudio.com

Bark Design Architects
>> 146

PO Box 1355
Noosa Heads, Queensland 4567
(Australia)
T +617.5471.0340
F +617.5471.0343
info@barkdesign.com.au
www.barkdesign.com.au

Bernardes+Jacobsen Arquitetura
>> 72

Alameda Gabriel Monteiro da Silva,
1310 - Jd. Paulistano
São Paulo, SP (Brazil)
T +55.11.3082.6834
F +55.11.3082.6834
contato@jacobsenarquitetura.com
www.jacobsenarquitetura.com

Gianni Botsford Architects
>> 52

83–84 Berwick Street
London W1F 8TS (United Kingdom)
T +44.7434.277
info@giannibotsford.com
www.giannibotsford.com

Choo Gim Wah Architect
>> 222

31-1, Jln Desa Cahaya 11, Tmn
Desa Bukit Cahaya
Cheras, 56000 KL, WP (Malaysia)
T +60.3.9105.6512
F +60.3.9105.6514
info@cgwarchitect.com
www.cgwarchitect.com

Atelier Sacha Cotture
>> 226

8f, Chemphil bldg, 851 Antonio
Arnaiz Av, Legaspi Village
Makati City, 1227 (Philippines)
T +63.511.8708
sacha@ateliersachacotture.com
www.ateliersachacotture.com

CR2 Architecture
>> 92

Rua Inácio Pereira da Rocha, 158
São Paulo, SP (Brazil)
T +55.11.3034.4484
cr2@cr2arquitetura.com.br
www.cr2arquitetura.com.br

Datumzero Design Office
>> 48

113 Cedar Street, loft 5C
New York, NY, 10006 (USA)
T +1.212.625.9640
F +1.212.346.9685
g.garita@datumzero.com
www.datumzero.com

Department of Architecture Co., Ltd.
>> 206

18th Fl. Smooth Life Building,
44 North Sathon Rd.
Bangrak, Bangkok 10500 (Thailand)
T +66.2.6339.936
F +66.2.6339.940
dept.of.arch@gmail.com
www.departmentofarchitecture.co.th

Martín Dulanto Sangalli
>> 64

Isabel Duprat
>> 96

**Elías Rizo Arquitectos – Elías Rizo
Suarez & Rizo Alejandro Suarez**
>> 40

Gral. Eulogio Parra 2802, col.
Providencia
Guadalajara, Jalisco (Mexico)
T +52.33.3632.1208
taller@eliasrizo.com
www.eliasrizo.com

Gil Fialho
>> 82

Rua Arthur de Azevedo, 636
05404-001 São Paulo (Brazil)
T +55.11.3062.4375
conteudo@gilfialho.com.br
www.gilfialho.com.br

Gonzalez Moix Architecture
>> 60

Raul Ferrero Avenue #1274, Office 8
La Molina (Peru)
T +51.1.637.5866
oscar@gonzalezmoix.com
www.gonzalezmoix.com

Natalia Heredia
>> 56

JC Arquitectura – Juan Carral
>> 32

jc@jcarquitectura.com.mx
www.jcarquitectura.com.mx

K2LD Architects
>> 190

261 Waterloo Street #02-32
Singapore 180261 (Singapore)
T +65.6738.7277
info@k2ld.com.sg
www.k2ld.com.sg

**Khosla Associates – Sandeep Khosla
& Amaresh Anand**
>> 154

No. 646, 1st D Main, Domlur Layout
Bangalore 560071, Karnataka
(India)
T +91.80.2535.3131
F +91.80.2535.8186
info@khoslaassociates.com
www.khoslaassociates.com

Mathias Klotz
>> 126

Los Colonos 041
Santiago (Chile)
T +56.2.223.3661
estudio@mathiasklotz.com
www.mathiasklotz.com

studio mk27 – Marcio Kogan
>> 82, 96

Alameda Tiete, 505 Jardins
01417-020 São Paulo, SP (Brazil)
T +55.11.3081.3522
info@studiomk27.com.br
www.studiomk27.com.br

Landmak Architecture, JSC
>> 218

R.1204, F.12, Buil.B10B, Nam Trung
Yen, District Cau Giay
Ha Noi (Vietnam)
T +84.4.6269.1866
vinh@landmak.vn
www.landmak.vn

Ney Lima
>> 68

SRTVS Qd. 701 Bl. O Sala 725
Ed. Centro Multiempresarial
70.340-000 Brasilia, DF (Brazil)
T +55.61.3225.2131
contato@neylima.com.br
www.neylima.com.br

**Luis Pons Design Lab –
Luis G. Pons**
>> 22

4040 NE 2nd Avenue, Loft 312
Moore Building
Miami, FL 33137 (USA)
T +1.305.576.1787
F +1.305.576.1788
info@luispons.com
www.luispons.com

Edgardo Minond
>> 126

El salvador 4753 PB C.P. 141
Buenos Aires (Argentina)
T +54.11.4833.3401
edgardo@minond.com.ar
www.minond.com.ar

MM++ Architects >> 214

103/6 Tran Ke Xuong , Ward 7,
Phu Nhuan District
Ho Chi Minh City (Vietnam)
T +84.8.3841.0550
F +84.8.3841.0550
mimya@mmarchitects.net
www.mmarchitects.net

P+o Architecture – David Pedroza Castañeda >> 36

T +52.811.933.7514
davidpedroz@gmail.com
www.dpc-arq.blogspot.mx

Silvio Rech & Lesley Carstens >> 142

T +27.82.900.9935
adventarch@mweb.co.za

Reyes Ríos + Larraín Arquitectos >> 28

Calle 49, # 510 C
Merida, Yucatan (Mexico)
T +52.999.928.7841
info@reyesrioslarrain.com
www.reyesrioslarrain.com

Sérgio Sampaio Arquitetura + Planejamento >> 102

Av. Prudente de morais, 210
Itu, SP (Brazil)
T +55.11.4025.1038
sergio@sergiosampaio.arq.br
www.sergiosampaio.arq.br

SAOTA – Stefan Antoni Olmesdahl Truen Architects >> 130, 136

109 Hatfield Street, Gardens
8001 Cape Town (South Africa)
T +27.21.468.4400
F +27.21.461.5408
info@saota.com
www.saota.com

Shigeru Ban Architects >> 198

5-2-4 Matsubara, Setagaya
Tokyo 156-0043 (Japan)
T +81.3.3324.6760
F +81.3.3324.6789
tokyo@shigerubanarchitects.com
www.shigerubanarchitects.com

M/s. SJK Architects >> 150

302 & 303, Veena Killedar Industrial Estate, 10-14 Pais Street
Byculla (W), Mumbai 400011 (India)
T +91.22.2300.8761
F +91.22.2309.0983
design@sjkarchitect.com
www.sjkarchitect.com

SO (Situation based Operation) – Narong Othavorn >> 202

200/2 Soi Phutha-o-soth Nares Rd.
Bangrak Bangkok 10500 (Thailand)
T +66.81.805.9300
F +66.2.618.5347
absoluts@mac.com

spbr arquitetos – Angelo Bucci >> 106

Faria Lima 1234, 121
01451 913 São Paulo, SP (Brazil)
T +55.11.3815.1171
spbr@spbr.arq.br
www.spbr.arq.br

SPG Architects >> 44

127 W 26th Street #800
New York, NY, 10001 (USA)
T +1.212.366.5500
F +1.212.366.6559
contact@spgarchitects.com
www.spgarchitects.com

Craig Steely Architecture >> 18

8 Beaver Street
San Francisco, CA 94114 (USA)
T +1.415.864.7013
F +1.415.864.7013
info@craigsteely.com
www.craigsteely.com

Max Strang Architecture >> 8

3326 Mary Street Suite 301
Miami, FL 33133 (USA)
T +1.305.373.4990
jason@strangarchitecture.com
www.strangarchitecture.com

Gisele Taranto Arquitetura >> 88

Rua J J Seabra 14 casa 2, Jardim Botânico
22470-130 Rio de Janeiro (Brazil)
T +55.21.2579.0448
gtarquitetura@gtarquitetura.com
www.giseletaranto.com

Studio Guilherme Torres >> 110, 122

Rua Francisco Leitão, 653. CJ.52
Sao Paulo, SP (Brazil)
T +55.11.2872.8620
info@guilhermetorres.com.br
www.guilhermetorres.com.br

Touzet Studio Inc. >> 12

65 NW 25th Street
Miami, FL 33127 (USA)
T +1.305.789.2870
F +1.305.789.2872
info@touzetstudio.com
www.touzetstudio.com

UNA Arquitetos >> 114

Rua General Jardim 770 cj.13a
01223-010 São Paulo, SP (Brazil)
T +55.11.3231.3080
F +55.11.3231.2526
una@unaarquitetos.com.br
www.unaarquitetos.com.br

Vo Trong Nghia Architects – Vo Trong Nghia, Daisuke Sanuki, Shunri Nishizawa >> 210

8F, 70 Pham Ngoc Thach street,
Ward 6, District 3
Ho Chi Minh City (Vietnam)
T +84.8.3820.6699
F +84.8.3820.8439
hcmc@vtnaa.com
www.votrongnghia.com

Wahana Architects – Rudy Kelana & Matheus Sompotan & Gerard Tambunan >> 166, 174

Jalan Ciputat Raya no. 351 Kebayoran Lama Utara
Jakarta Selatan 12240 (Indonesia)
T +62.21.7279.3419
F +62.21.7279.3417
info@wahanaarchitects.com
www.wahanaarchitects.com

Wallflower Architecture + Design >> 194

7500A Beach Rd #15-303 The Plaza
Singapore 199591 (Singapore)
T +65.6297.6883
admin@wallflower.com.sg
www.wallflower.com.sg

Word of Mouth – Valentina Audrito >> 170

Jl. Pantai Berawa, Gang 22
Banjar Tandeg, Canggu, Kuta Utara,
Bali (Indonesia)
T +62.361.844.6168
F +62.361.844.6168
info@wordofmouthbali.com
www.wordofmouthbali.com

Picture Credits

Alan Abraham	158–161
Patrick Bingham Hall	190–193
Edgard Cesar	68–71
Sofia Flores Chapa	36–39
Bruce Damonte	18–21
Datumzero design office	48–51
Wacho Espinosa	32–35
Leonardo Finotti	72–77, 102–105, 114–117, 118–121
Marcos García	40–43
Fernando Gomulya	166–169, 174–177
Fernando Guerra	82–87, 96–101
Happy Lim Photography	162–165
Edward Hendricks, CI & A Photography	178–181
Robin Hill	12–17
Hiroyuki Hirai	198–201
Andrew Howard, courtesy of Wilderness Safaris	142–145
Christopher Frederick Jones	146–149
Sanjay Kewlani	182–185, 186–189
Nelson Kon	106–109
Le Anh Duc	218–221
Adam Letch	136–141
Kenneth Lim of Gray Studio, Malaysia	222–225
Charles Lindsay	44–47
Denilson Machada (MCA Estúdio)	110–113, 122–125
Claudio Manzoni	126–129
MCA Estúdio	88–91
Rafaela Netto	92–95
Juan Solano Ojasi	60–63
Hiroyuki Oki	210–213, 214–217
Shamanth Patil	154–157
Christian Richters	52–55
SAOTA & Adam Letch	130–135
Pim Schalkwijk	28–31
Marco Simola	64–67
Edward Simon	226–229
SO & Piyawut Srisakul	202–205
Moch. Sulthonn	170–173
Gerard Tessier	22–27
Marc Tey	194–197
Wison Tungthunya	206–209
Claudia Uribe-Touri	8–11
David Uribe	56–59
Rajesh Vora	150–153
Word of Mouth	171 a. l.

All other pictures, especially plans, were made available by
the architects and/or designers.